CW00662236

*This book is dedicated
to my 18-year-old self,
who would never believe
how much they would
have achieved.*

1.Hating my own body.

my body
my temple
ruins of my past
white lines around my thighs
showing my mistakes
why am I like this?
why do I keep repeating
the same mistakes?
am I a mistake?
am I the problem?
or is it society
brainwashing me;
crushing my soul;
pushing me on my knees
above the toilet seat
puking it all out
crying my soul out
oh, how much
i loathe myself

head, ears, back, knees
everything hurts
i am going to collapse
then i realise it's her
visiting me again
it's the monthly date
that i can't escape
i used to be so afraid of the blood
at its sight i would act hysterical
faint, cry, scream
but now
now i have made peace
with my period
but i'm still fighting with the pain;
the pain that leaves me paralysed in my bed
crying my eyes out
no matter how many painkillers i take
i feel like a living dead
barely able to walk
blood runs down my thighs
constant headaches
lifeless lying in my bed
begging for some help
counting the days to pass by

my hips are so large
why is my stomach not flat?
why do i think losing weight
will make me instantly happy?
thus, i won't eat anything today
oh god
i am starving
i need to eat
but
i do not deserve it
why is loving your body hard?
why can i not be happy in it
i feel every piece of this chocolate i ate in my glutes
giving me more cellulite
making me larger
oh god
i hate myself

sitting in front of the mirror
examining every inch of fat
touching my hairy legs
tears running down my cheeks
and like that
without me realising
my fists hit the mirror
broken glass everywhere
blood running from my hands
but i can not stop
knees collapsing hard on the floor
my mind hurts more than
my bleeding hands
removing shards of glass
from my hands carefully
tears running hot down my cheeks
i get up slowly
wiping the blood from hands to my body
i am standing there
on top of the broken glasses
my fat belly, my thick full-of-cellulite thighs
covered in blood
swollen eyes, red nose, wet lips
wet cheeks, eyes shut
i can not live like this anymore

2.Fighting with my mind.

i have always been a prisoner
of my mind
i can not escape the thoughts
no matter how hard i try
no matter what i do
anxiety creeps in my limbs
they are shaking
i am sweating
chest struggles for air
i can not bear living
like this
anymore

sitting on the floor naked
hugging my knees tightly
blood is dripping from my wrists
face buried between my thighs
sobbing my heart out
painkillers can not help
the pain in my head
my mind is constantly focusing
on the knife
that is conveniently on the floor
close to my right hip
but I am too much of a coward
to finish me

and i keep falling,
again, and again,
in depression's trap
i can't leave my bed
sleeping has become my partner
i have no interest in leaving my room
taking showers has become harder and harder
i don't feel my limbs anymore
migraines, stomach ache and nausea
are my best friends
nothing makes me happy
and
i am lost once again

silence has scared me
since i was a kid
thoughts are getting loud
they terrify me
they bully me
they patronize me
they whisper one thing to me
commit the perfect suicide
paint the walls with your blood
create the most beautiful death
as you are not a piece of art,
but your death can be
this whisper is in my head
24/7
non-stop
to harm myself
to end me
to make a bloody mess
my death should be a piece of art
the perfect bloodbath

thinking of running away again
every time i find myself in a difficult situation
i feel the only way out is just leaving
i feel like i want to disappear
just pack some personal belongings
sell my phone
buy a new phone
and leave
just disappear
don't have any plans
don't have any place in mind
no place can hide my sadness
no place can bear my darkest thoughts
just a great need to leave
to travel
to be someone else
to be anywhere
and everywhere
that will be enough for a while
and maybe i will be able to disappear for ever
and maybe i will become the greatest missing case

i sit and watch people passing by
some walk fast
some seem lost
while others dance and sing
in the middle of the street
and then there's me
alone
wondering if
i am the only one who questions
the meaning of life
am i the only one who doesn't fit in?
am i the only one who worries too much?
am i the only one who overthinks?
am i the only one that gets sick of
repeating the same long, energy - draining
routine
day after day
i want to crawl into my bed
and cry my lungs out
and scream into the endless void

my lungs are stretching out
opening wide
silence
no crying
no more tears
left to shed
my throat is blocked
my voice is gone
nothing is left to say
just an unbearable pain in my soul;
it will leave a stain
forever
that's what i am thinking
while i am grabbing a pillow
to hug in the hopes
of sleeping
but my weeping doesn't let me
sadness has overtaken me
my soul
my body
my brain
i am becoming sadness

eyes wide like berries
looking the ceiling
my mind is lost
a chaos of thoughts
tired of the same voices
visiting me every night
creeping on me
bothering me
like debt collectors
things i did
things i didn't do
and i am still here
lying on my kitchen floor
wondering what the fuck is wrong with me

there are some days
that are different than the others
that just don't feel right
nothing specific happened
no arguments
no difficult decisions were taken
no hardships
just some days feel meh
and i don't know how to describe
this feeling
of emptiness inside of me
nothing can fulfil me
not even my favourite food
not even my favourite movie
not even my lover's face
just need to lie in my bed
in silence
watching pointless videos
counting the seconds passing by
with my lover's hands wrapped around me
yes that's what i want on meh days

breaking points
emotional breakdowns
one back to another
leaving me exhausted
crying in my kitchen floor
letting all my sadness
drown me
waves of tears above my head
i can not breathe
i close my eyes
and i enter the realm of darkness

i am dying slowly
every day that passes by
every hour
every minute
every second
is
another step closer
to my
graveyard stone

there are some moments
when i picture my suicide
in my head
leaving clues behind
describing my pain
every detail well-planned
oh...
i find so much peace
in these thoughts.
how ironic!

days like this
i do not want to leave my bed
days like this
i am dragging my body around my house
days like this
i am sitting at the desk
in front of my laptop, i can't do any work
i am so unmotivated, unproductive, thus
i feel useless
there are also other days when i am happy
i am content beyond words, when i can do anything
i feel like wonder woman
i can conquer the whole world

3.Innocence is gone.

looking up
looking down
standing on the edge of the roof
just a step away from my death
what if.....?
i just jump
looking down
looking up
my right leg is up
my heart is beating fast
looking down
getting dizzy
i collapse on the roof
looking up
sun is bright
it is another beautiful day
to put on my fake smile
and continue my miserable life

sitting on my toilet seat
with my pants on
smoking cigarettes non-stop
my breath stinks of alcohol
head is spinning
tons of cigarette buds on the floor
i am in a trance
looking for more ways
to destroy myself
putting out the cigarettes on my thighs
burning my cellulite away
burning my fat, disgusting things
pouring alcohol on the wounds
the more i feel pain, the less i think
of hurting myself
so i need to keep hurting;
slapping my face
nose bleeding
laughing maniacally
room spinning around me
cigarettes, alcohol, pills, blood
i collapse on the floor

another sleepless night
mind is getting sicker and sicker
body starts rotting
muscles pain
leg feels numb
"νους υγιής εν σώματι υγιεί"
"in corpore sano"
"a healthy mind in a healthy body"
but
my mind is rotten
full of maggots
eating my brain
destroying my memories
i can not leave my bed
i can not open my eyes
mouth is dry
no more tears left to cry
can not speak
my body has given up
and i just lie there still
just breathing

i live in my head
i do not know how to exist
out of my head
the line between
fantasy and reality is so thin
i wish i was living in a video game
i wouldn't have to make any decisions then
what if we live in a simulation though?
what if nothing is real?
what if we are just pawns in God's hands?

i am kind
and you abused it
you asked for help
so i lost myself
helping you in any way i could
you kept asking for more and more
i couldn't give more
i am empty
asking for some space
i need to breathe
you grabbed me violently
dragging me along the floor
you got me on my knees
my mind blacked out
my mouth went sore
i am paralysed
while you are standing there
with your pants down
and then
you took my innocence

i am very open to talking about those;
those ones who stole my innocence
those who took a piece of my soul
those who i still see in my nightmares
their names are forgotten
but their faces are still clear in my head
revisiting the monstrosities
trying to act brave
trying not to show any sign
but sometimes i lose
sometimes they win
again
sometimes i get lost in the dark hole
and i am falling;
failing till
i manage to find the strength to
stand up on my feet again

sitting in the sun
with my bare hairy legs
wearing my favourite bikini
listening to some music;
minding my own business
then i notice a shadow
in front of me
i look up and i see
the face of a very hungry man
looking at my bosom
like he wants to devour me
like he has been starving his whole life

and i can not help thinking
when will men stop harassing me?
when will men stop thinking i exist
for their own entertainment?
when will men stop thinking that my body
exists for their sick fantasies?
immediately i get up and leave
embarrassed even knowing
i am not wrong
my body is not wrong
i am not responsible
for how other people perceive me
i wish one day i won't be embarrassed
i wish one day i won't feel ashamed
i wish one day i can stand my ground
i wish one day i will be brave

sometimes i feel numb
sometimes i feel sad
sometimes i feel pessimistic
sometimes i feel anxious
sometimes i feel stressed
and sometimes i feel nothing at all
then i know that
the despair is near
i can hear it coming
louder and louder
footsteps are at my door
not knocking at the door
just bursting in
hitting me hard
throwing me on the floor
leaving me squealing from agony
the only thing on my mind
i can't cope anymore
i want to end me

depression is the demon
lurking behind my soul's secret door
always waiting
for the right moment
to visit me and scare me
making me frightened
of my own life
reminding me how insignificant i am
how stupid i am
how meaningless i am
dragging me with force from my feet
not sure how to win
no matter what
i always fail

they say life is fun
i should be happy
being alive
but they do not know
the lies my brain tells me
how much it makes me think
i do not deserve life
i do not deserve to breathe
i only deserve death
a slow painful one;
i mean
no one cares anyway

sleepless nights
dreaming away
things will never happen
i do not know how to make them happen
i can not stop wondering
if i am talented enough
or if i am just a failure
will i ever succeed
or will i die trying ?
thoughts make my head spin
throb
leaving me unable to close my eyes
my nightmares are here alive
torturing me
draining my energy
they leave me helpless

breathing in
breathing out
struggling for
some air
lying on the bathroom floor
listening to muffling sounds
people walking
chatting
eating
and i am just lying there
in my workplace's bathroom floor
trying to remove my clothes
unclasping my bra
my ribs hurt
my eyes are red
my lips turn white
no colour in my cheeks either
my whole body is fighting for some air
and then
the air finally manages to hit my lungs
my whole body shakes trying to
get as much air as possible
breaths get faster and faster
till the world stops spinning around
i return to reality

carrying a suitcase full of hopes and dreams
taking the plane
without any plans
with a few bucks in my pocket
sleeping in the cold floor of the airport
waiting for the next flight
upon arrival
i am shocked
with this new world
by this new adventure that awaits me
feeling tired and exhausted
decided to stay at this station
sleeping on the bench
my belly feels peckish
but i ignore it
that is a tomorrow problem

i am in despair
trying to find someone
to connect with me
to fall in love with me
to get me
to love all of me; even my flaws
but today's relationships
are superficial
human connections are rare
but
i am a hopeless romantic
i fall in love easily
and thus i break my heart

since i was young
i knew
i knew i didn't fit in
with the people around me
in the society i grew up
i felt like an alien
i wish i had the right words
i felt like the black sheep
my critical thoughts,
my beliefs
my personality
were beyond this society's borders
i couldn't connect
with anyone
i was surrounded by friends,
relatives, schoolmates, co-workers
and i felt alone;
the kind of loneliness
that kills you day by day

hot water
running from above
burning my hair
my scalp
i do not care
i am on my knees
unable to stand
unable to move
i want the world to stop
so i can breathe
i feel lost
overthinking makes me dizzy
my eyes are red
hot tears running from my eyes
and i just exist there
maybe for a couple of minutes
maybe for a couple of hours
i do not know
my feet and hands are numb
my skin is burnt
but i do not care
i just go to bed
all wet
just wanting to sleep

one more sleepless night
lying down
breathing heavy
my mind refuses to shut down
thoughts are dancing wild
around my brain
my body is filled with despair
it needs some sleep
but my mind
makes me get up
dancing wildly
crying my eyes out
exhausting myself
praying my body will collapse
so that i can sleep

i am a master of hiding my pain
with a smile
i have 10 years of experience
i keep making the same mistakes
giving my energy to the wrong things
then i end up more broken than before

eyes wide open
questioning what is happening
hands tied unwillingly
my veins struggling to get free
legs moving frantically
the friction with the rope
burns my ankles
is this a dream or not?

4.Healing my scars.

i love myself
i love myself for all the times
i've been crying until i fell asleep
i love myself for all the times
i've been lost in my thoughts
i love myself for all the times
i've been deceived and
for all the times i have been laughed at
i love myself for the way i stutter
when I try to claim something i want
i love myself because i am clumsy
i love myself even though i could have said a lot,
but i didn't
i love myself for all the opportunities
i have missed.
i love myself for all the times
i have kept my temper
i love myself for all the dreams
i have dreamed
i love myself for all the times
i let myself be fooled
i love myself for all the weird faces
i can pull
i love myself for all the times
i tried to be something i'm not

i love myself for all the embarrassing
and awkward moments
that i have endured
i love myself for how easily
get attached to people
i love myself for my naivety
and my innocence
i love myself for my loud
and annoying laugh
i love myself for my big smile
i love myself for my badly shaped nose
i love myself for all the times
no-one else showed me love
but most importantly,
i love myself for all the times
i defended myself
for all the times i have been humiliated,
but i proved them wrong
for all the times
i made them shut their mouths
for all the times i fought and won
and even if no-one loves me,
then i will love myself more,
damn!

days like these
i feel care-free
i go out
the sun kisses my pale cheeks
making them blush
the wind plays innocently with my hair
the scent of the flowers
awaking my urge of running
freely
across the fields
tumbling on the ground
and becoming one with the earth

30 days passed
no plan
with survival mode on
exploring the city
applying for any kind of job
eating one meal per day
sleeping on the cold floor of the station
feeling hopeful
even though
i have nothing
it's crazy how unsafe
unloved
unprotected
i felt in my family's home
in my own homeland
i seek love in a foreign country
without any plan
and
i made it

on my 18th birthday
i decided to embrace my real identity
cutting my hair short
and dyeing it orange
getting my nose pierced
and getting my first tattoo
buying more masculine clothes
checking myself out
in the mirror and
i am finally seeing who i wanna be
in my reflection
if only you could see
the big smile on my face

things i used to hate about myself but not anymore:
my belly
acne on my face
my big ears
my frizzy hair
my weird-shaped eyebrows
my conical sagging boobs
my funny-looking labia
my love handles
my thick thighs
my tiny fingers

i am in love with myself,
the white lines on my breasts
the white lines on my thighs
they look like tattoos
my collarbones look like
ones of a statue
and my garden is rich and ready
ready for my touch
i was embarrassed to touch myself
i thought it was a sin
but how can i fall in love with myself
if i don't make love to myself ?
i explore all the curves, trying to learn
what i like, how i like it
and like that i am falling in love with myself

i contradict myself all the time
i feel my body is my eternal home
i need to love and take care of it
with all its flaws
i should not be complaining if it works properly
i can walk
i can use my hands
i can see
i can smell
i can feel
but
there are moments
when i can not help wondering
how great i would feel if i was skinnier
or if my ears weren't that big
or if my belly was flat

and here i am again
standing in front of the mirror
naked and vulnerable
checking myself out
touching my boobs
properly feeling them
testing what feels right
what makes them aroused
my fingers are going down
to my secret garden
am i attracted to girls?
or am i a boy?
these thoughts
have troubled my head
for a while now
internal homophobia,
lack of proper sex and gender education,
self-hatred was the reason i was struggling
i was struggling to accept and love myself

coming to terms with my sexuality
was a long, anguishing road
now reflecting back on my teenage years
i can now admit that
i was madly in love with one of my teachers
she was the most beautiful woman
i have ever laid my eyes on
back then i was scared, confused,
terrified of the way my heart was beating
every time i saw her,
the way she made me so happy
being in her presence
i just wish that i knew
these feelings were normal
back then and that
i didn't have to carry this
internalised guilt
i wish i knew being attracted to women is okay
i wish i knew i wasn't a freak

since when did i become so harsh on myself?
since when did i forget to love me?
how can i go back on loving me?
then i decided to take myself on a date
i put on my favourite pants,
and this shirt that made me look good
i did my hair, my make-up,
my favourite book in hand
and i went to the park
lying down, feeling the fresh air on my face,
reading my book, enjoying the sun
inhaling all the beautiful smells of the flowers
and i take time to be present
at that moment i am in love with myself

i do not fit society's beauty standards
i loathe shaving; i enjoy having hairy legs,
hairy armpits, i seriously do not care
it's just hair so why do people care?
i loathe wearing dresses and skirts;
wearing a dress makes me feel
like a fish out of water
as formal outfit i always choose a suit
i feel comfortable and sexy in it
i am tired of trying to fit beauty standards,
when i can just be me

letting myself relax
not be productive
all the time
is a thing i can't do
i don't know how
i always feel the pressure
to create something
to be successful
to be useful
i wish i could make myself get lost in the moment
and just exist
i sometimes wish i could lie down in my bed
looking the ceiling
focusing on my breath
worrying about nothing
and just existing in this peaceful moment
i wish for some silence in my head

asking for help is hard
when i have asked for help in the past
people have mocked me
calling me crazy
telling me there is nothing wrong with me
i just need to relax and everything will be fine
they don't believe how much i struggle
even when i am standing there
with dark circles under my eyes,
with cuts in my wrists and all over my body
when i tell them all the million ways
i have thought of ending my life
they just sit there and judge me
till one person finally believed me
and offered to help me
without judgement
and at that moment
i crumbled
i cried so hard then;
i cried because someone believed me
and wanted to help
asking for help is hard
but it's worth to give it a try

sun kissing my toes
highlighting the hair in my big toes
my old self would be ashamed
and disgusted
my old self would leave immediately
to go and hide themselves
back to the house
to remove the hair
but my now-self is thankful
for this body;
my legs carry me around
i can explore the whole world
my chubby arms help me
write, read, clean
my skinny fingers let me touch
and sense everything around me
my now - self is in love with their body
and that's the most beautiful love story

my teenage self could never imagine
this version of myself
being so carefree
not caring about other people's opinions
leaving the house unshaved
in my buggy pyjamas, without any makeup
walking like i am the Queen
at the age of 28,
i am in love with my full of cellulite thick thighs,
my small and weak arms,
my round boobs and my acne-prone face
and this is the best love story of all time

5.Miscellaneous.

Like Emmeline
submitted to Digital Arts Festival
14-21/6/2021

Emmeline fought to have her voice heard
So I decided to raise mine
To say how society mistreated me
I thought men and women had equal rights
I thought women's voices mattered
as much as men's do
But I was wrong
I was crazy to believe that
those who mistreated me
would change
and would accept me
and would listened to me
respectfully
When I opened my soul
worldwide and shared
the abuse i received from men
expecting them to realise their mistakes
and apologise

But I was wrong
My voice didn't matter
And Like Emmeline I was punished
for raising my voice
demanding equal treatment
But they pointed their fingers at me
because I am a woman
But like Emmeline I kept fighting
and demanding equal rights
My name is Sky
and I demand to have my voice heard
so I can share all the ways
society let me down
and hurt my soul permanently
and share my thoughts on
how to improve the future
Like Emmeline, I am a fighter
Like Emmeline, I won't give up
Like Emmeline,
I am going to fight for all women

For Her

the first thing i noticed about her
was her full-of-life brown eyes
looking at me so curiously
looking at everything new
so delightful
so bright
brighter than the sun itself,
then i noticed her freckles
all over her face
like the stars in the sky
i wanted to kiss all of them
lose count and start again
so i can spend my whole life
worshiping her
then it was her smile
i have never seen a more beautiful smile
shining prouder than sun
so how could i avoid
falling for her?
especially when
she came into my life
at the right time to save me

she is the one i know
that i want to travel with
go on adventures
lie in bed with
forever
arms entangled
messy hair
sweaty bodies
thighs suffocating each other
there
she is my safe place
and i am hers
her
it's all about her
all the love i have
it's for her
all the admiration i have
it's for her
all of my breaths
it's for her

shivering
trembling
eyes shut
left hand holding the sheet tightly
sweat rolling down between my boobs
hips jerking back and forth
right hand exploring all the right places
that can make me come undone

i only felt real love in her eyes
i only felt safe in her arms
i only found God when
she touched my sacred garden
love like this can not be considered a sin
love like this can not be considered disgusting
love like this is real
love like this is precious

my first time with a woman
was messy, chaotic and full of laughter
i only knew what to do from the lesbian movies
i had seen
i kissed her collarbone, her breasts;
i ran my tongue along her body till
i landed in her secret garden
i devoured her smell, her arousal
i was intoxicated and let myself get lost there
my tongue obsessed by her sweet juices
my ears falling in love with her sweet moans
she was calling my name in such a divine way;
i think I found God
asi was giving her the first orgasm,
i felt myself cumming too
just like that, so simple
my first time with a woman
taught me you don't need physical touch
for pleasure; this love feels too good
to be considered wrong; this love feels real
and so natural

Made in the USA
Columbia, SC
21 November 2022

71225188R00037